The Key Questions

for Business Partners

Also Available from Wise Counsel Press

How to Train Your Clients to Pay You

(audio + workbook)

Term$ and Condition$: Ten Steps to

Increasing Your Returns from Your Small Business Agreements

"The Fine Print" for Small Businesses:

Ten Steps to Using "Boilerplate" to Avoid Unnecessary Lawsuits

Getting The Best From Working With Attorneys

(PDF special report)

The Key Questions

for Business Partners

100 Vital Questions to Ask
Before Going into Business with Someone Else

Nina L. Kaufman

iUniverse, Inc.
New York   Lincoln   Shanghai

The Key Questions for Business Partners
100 Vital Questions to Ask Before Going into
Business with Someone Else

iUniverse books may be ordered through booksellers or by
contacting:

iUniverse
2021 Pine Lake Road, Suite 100
Lincoln, NE 68512
www.iuniverse.com
1-800-Authors (1-800-288-4677)

ISBN: 978-0-595-44507-3 (pbk)
ISBN: 978-0-595-88834-4 (ebk)

Printed in the United States of America

general legal concepts or requirements. You should always confirm with your attorney whether the information contained in this book applies to your state and situation.

Wise Counsel Press LLC

New York

To my husband, Joe Carr

A true partner, in every sense of the word,

who helps me "keep the faith"

CONTENTS

The Key Questions

PREFACE

Years ago, I had a collaborative partnership in the filmmaking business ... to the extent that a trio of eight-year-olds could even call it that. I was the would-be actress and screenwriter; Larin, the wannabe director and cinematographer; Eric, the set designer (and occasional lead vampire). Week after week, we would make silly five-minute films, set in the dark dungeon that was Larin's basement, strewn with sofa cushions, old bed sheets, and lamps held at odd angles by Larin's baby sisters. Each 8mm opus was an answer to the questions, "What do we want to do? How can we make it work?" Each movie was a journey, an exploration into something new and creative that brought abundant joy (and many giggles) to each one of us.

This book is filled with questions. Each one is a journey to be savored, not just for the answers that you will glean, but for the person you will become for having taken it. As the sales guru Og Mandino once wrote, "Take the attitude of a student. Never be too big to ask questions; never know too much to learn something new." May *The Key Questions* help you find the right partners for your business—ones who will challenge you and support you in a spirit of integrity, fun, and abundance.

A friendship founded on business is a good deal better than a business founded on friendship.

—John D. Rockefeller

INTRODUCTION

Dean arrived at the office thinking it would be a Friday like any other. He had spent every week of the past two months flying back and forth to Los Angeles as partner and lead counsel on the *Driscoll* case, leaving home Monday nights to be in L.A. for the Tuesday 10:00 a.m. calendar call of Judge Groban, and taking the Thursday red-eye back to New York City to contend with law firm administration and other matters on Fridays. Not much time or energy for family, but this is what the business required—and his partners demanded.

It was still a bit early, so the office wasn't exactly bustling. Dean's firm was known in the litigation business as a "young upstart". Many of the partners had come from other prestigious Wall Street firms. Having become disillusioned—or impatient—with the politics and years of servitude it took to get recognition and "make partner," the attorneys broke off and founded their own firm. Immediately, clients flooded through their doors, because of their reputation as hard and clever litigators. They were the go-to firm if you wanted to sue the pants off another company and bring it to its knees. Foreign clients, who wouldn't stand for that kind of litigiousness in their home countries, loved it in America—and paid highly for it, too. *Are we that far removed from the gun-slinging Wild West?* Dean wondered in passing. Very quickly, the firm had developed a strong reputation and loyal following. The partners rewarded themselves and their hard work with windowed offices in a prime downtown Manhattan location. Dean sometimes questioned the real need for this extra overhead, but the clients loved the panoramic views of lower Manhattan, the Statue of Liberty, Ellis Island, and other landmarks. It made them feel as if they were in the hands of those who had power and control. And, Dean had to admit, there was always something soothing about walking past the conference rooms, steaming hot coffee in hand, and seeing the sunlight shimmering and dappling on the river. Something Zen-like, something grand, he felt. He would pause for a moment as he walked past, and take a deep breath. The view helped him both to clear his mind and to focus, which is why he liked to walk past it on the way back to his office.

But that Friday, instead of the pristine view of the water, he saw his partners huddled inside the conference room. Some were gesticulating wildly and shouting; others were slumped in their seats and looked ashen. Whatever it was, it wasn't the congenial boisterousness that Dean had come to expect from his colleagues. Dean opened the door and asked, "What's going on here?"

"Oh, good ... glad you're back," one responded. "We weren't sure when your plane got in. We've got a problem."

"You sure as s**t can say that again," another retorted.

Yelling and arguing continued in the background. "I'll sue that motherf——!!" "Yeah?!? With whose money?!?"

"Well, is someone going to tell me what's going on?" Dean asked.

One partner sat, nearly immobile, with his elbows on the polished mahogany conference room table, his head in his hands. He hardly flinched when a partner sitting next to him hit the table with his fist, uttering an expletive.

"Go on, tell him. You found out first!" chimed in another.

The first partner took a deep breath. He gazed out the window at the sparkling river, as if taking it in for one last time, looked at Dean gravely, and intoned, time then looked at Dean gravely, and intoned, "Hugh [the managing partner] walked off with the operating account. We're broke."

It's stories like Dean's that make most business owners prefer to stick burning needles in their eyes than bring another owner into their companies. "Business partners? What a headache!" they say, believing the burdens outweigh the benefits. Understandably, fears abound. Largely because—try as we might—we can never completely control another person. Our fears conjure up bleak pictures of failure, theft, disloyalty, bankruptcy. Here are some examples:

- My partner will walk off with all of the money

- My partner will walk off with our clients, and leave me with nothing
- My partner will get lazy and I'll have to do all of the work to keep the business afloat
- A partner will force me to take the company in a direction I don't want
- My partner will "cheat on me" and open a competing business
- Just when I'll get used to working with a partner, he or she will leave the business, which will leave me in the lurch
- My partner will steal my ideas
- My partner will turn out to be unstable and I won't be able to get rid of him or her
- Disagreements with my partner will destroy the company

The reasons can become as varied as the entrepreneurs themselves. Many of these fears can be kept in check with a good partnership agreement.

But equally compelling are the reasons *for* working with a business partner ... not the least of which is the value of collaboration. Rare is the entrepreneur who can achieve great heights totally and completely on his or her own. Even the inventor Thomas Edison, whom people often envision as toiling away alone in his laboratory into the wee hours, needed the help of employees, financiers, and collaborative partners to develop things we now take for granted: the incandescent light bulb, the motion picture camera, the phonograph (although antiquated, now), and electric lighting. In short, you can't reach your fullest potential in a vacuum. Your success depends, in part, on your ability to develop a strong team that will help you achieve your goals and guide you toward success. A business partner can be a vital part of that team.

After 11 years as an entrepreneur, business partner, and lawyer, I can say that I can heartily recommend business partnerships—provided you think them through carefully. There *is* a middle ground between Pollyanna and paranoia. Partnership is a journey that you take with yourself *and* with your business partner(s). I have had opportunities for growth and creative self-expression that I might never have had had I tried to go it alone. I have learned volumes about collaboration and working with people, which makes me a more effective "boss" and leader. And I have been blessed with a ready support system—a cheerleader to encourage me to stretch myself, a teammate to help puzzle through client- and entrepreneurship challenges, a jokester to buoy my moods, and a colleague with whom I can share my personal frustrations and fears about the impact of an entrepreneurial life upon myself and my family.

As a result of our long collaboration (which began well before we started our business together), I can honestly say that my law partner, Ron, is still among my top 5 favorite people to have lunch with on a regular basis. "Lunch? Who cares about lunch?" you ask. Lunch is significant: it means that I enjoy Ron's company. It means that I respect what he has to say. It means that I continue to feel I can learn from him, and he from me, even after all this time. "Lunch" reflects a continuing commitment to each other to help our business grow.

However, before I became a business partner, I first had to overcome my own obstacles to becoming an entrepreneur—as well as my own fears of partnership, which grew from the partner horror shows I had seen. My journey took place in the context of law and law firms. Don't let that background throw you. I could just as easily describe the journey of a "young apprentice" in any other service-based business: a public relations company; a marketing firm; another professional practice (dentistry, medical, chiropractic); a graphic design business; and so on. What I learned on the path from employee to partner helped me make the right choice—even though I didn't realize it at the time—by showing me exactly what I *didn't* want and would not accept.

My Journey to Partnership

The first time my business partner, Ron, asked me to join his law practice, I said no. I liked Ron and had enjoyed working with him at my first law firm. But the *last* thing I wanted to be was entrepreneurial. I had had visions of sugarplums and large law firm salaries dancing in my head since the time I had gone to law school. The idea of practicing law without an army of support staff flummoxed me. It was inconceivable! I mean, I knew people did it. There are far more sole practitioners in the country than those who work for large firms—48% of all lawyers, versus 14%. Still, I held onto the safety net of working for others. "Small firm" conjured up images of country lawyers along the lines of Gregory Peck and Jimmy Stewart characters, whom I did not see as entrepreneurial. Honorable, yes; wise, yes; but entrepreneurial? Boring work, no pizzazz, and old loafers came to mind.

Moreover, I had been taught that entrepreneurship was an option of "last resort". You work for yourself when no one else will hire you. Far better it is to work for a company/law firm that can provide you with a nice salary, benefits, and name recognition, so that you can say with pride that you've made it. Entrepreneurship came with all sorts of ugly labels, not the least of which was that if you subjected your family to your erratic income and earnings, you were morally and financially irresponsible. (Such was my mother's lesson from her entrepreneur father). And who wanted to be labeled as irresponsible? So I continued to labor for other law firms as an associate attorney.

The second time Ron asked me to join his law practice, I at least hesitated before saying no. Although I still wasn't ready to make the leap onto an entrepreneurial path, I was starting to come to terms with the realities of the law business. Reality wasn't pretty. The reverberations of stock- and real-estate market busts had rippled through the legal community. Competition for jobs—*any* job in the field—was fierce. Forget the promise of a six-figure salary to offset the accumulated six-figure law school debt. Abandon the status fantasies of working for a prestigious firm. Law firms had radically tightened their belts, and in many cases, had hiring freezes.

I had been one of the lucky ones to have employment after law school graduation. It was a tiny (by New York City standards), 3-partner firm in midtown Manhattan. At the time, I just wanted to be sure I had a job. But a job was all I had; no future. I worked 12-14 hours a day (for 1/3 of a Wall Street salary), and was expected to work every weekend. I had even been taken to task for not billing any time over a Thanksgiving weekend (yes, work was expected, even on a holiday). I had no prospects for advancement, certainly no promise of partnership (the pinnacle of achievement, for many lawyers), no meaningful opportunity to learn advanced lawyering skills like handling trial preparation and arguments. In some cases, the ethics of the partners I dealt with over the years crossed the line to out-and-out perjury. I had no opportunity to develop a client base; yet, the rungs to success were increasingly based upon the business you brought into a firm.

Especially when it came to partners, I saw all sorts of ugly aspects of that business relationship. I encountered partnerships with gross inequities: one partner had 99% of the ownership; the other had only 1% and yet was embarrassingly servile, like a Stepford wife. There were partners indicted for money laundering, which brought some of the other partners under investigation. There were partners who let slip snide comments about their colleagues like an unhappily married couple that won't divorce, showing an overall lack of respect. As a result, I had real misgivings about partnerships: *I continue to work like a dog, possibly get the short end of the stick in business ownership, run the risk of others' ethical shortcuts tainting me,* and *get the privilege of working with two-faced colleagues? This is what awaits me?* It didn't do much to endear me to the idea of becoming a partner in a small firm.

Gradually, though, I reached the point where the pain of staying in the same place grew greater than my fear of making a change. I remember sitting by the boulder-filled beach of Rockport, Massachusetts (during a rare weekend away to attend a friend's wedding), watching the waves crash against the shore. Every working day had been filled with anxiety and stress. My assumptions and fantasies about the big firm life had crashed and burned. Having seen so many lawyers get passed over for partnership, even after putting in thousands of billable hours per year, I began to question whether I really wanted that kind of back-breaking lifestyle. To expend all that time, to forego so many other things—vacations, time with family, other relationships—and then to be told in 8-12 years, "Thank you very much, Ms. Kaufman, but your services are no longer needed" was not exactly what I wanted to look forward to, especially when I wasn't seeing women stay at these various firms long enough to become partners.

Whether a "glass ceiling" or the work environment was discouraging women with families from staying, all I knew was that I had no role models to help me navigate my way to discover how to have it all—the brilliant career and the full family life—or at least to do my best in both worlds.

As I sat by the beach, a newer and bolder set of assumptions and values emerged. The still, small voice within, which I had suppressed for so long, made its presence known: "There *is* a better way," it said. I wanted an environment of my own choosing. I awoke to wanting control over my own destiny.

The third time Ron asked me to join his law practice, I agreed ... conditionally. I wanted to be sure I wasn't jumping from the frying pan into the fire. I had had enough resistance to overcome even to *consider* being a business owner that I *absolutely* did not want to become entangled in a partnership situation that I could not easily leave. But luckily, and unknowingly, with Ron I had stumbled upon several key factors in successful partnerships. First, Ron and I had worked together previously. As a result, I had had an opportunity to see him interact with other employees, with support staff, with clients. In Ron, I found an enthusiastic teacher, one willing to share his knowledge. Ron believed (and still does) that knowledge is not meant to be hoarded, that a candle's flame does not become diminished by lighting another candle. Other attorneys I had encountered were either competitive (not giving me all of the information I needed to figure out a problem) or uninvolved ("don't bother me; go figure it out yourself"). That desire to share, to mentor, to guide, is an important part of *values*, as we'll see more in Chapter 5. In addition, despite the bulldog litigiousness of trial law, Ron never resorted to browbeating tactics—with anyone. He treated all people with gentle respect, from the file clerk to opposing counsel to the presiding judge. What Ron didn't express in intimidation tactics and histrionics at trial, he more than made up for in intelligent trial strategy. And when opposing counsel got out of hand, he tended to put them in their place with a withering comment, rather than insults and epithets. Treating people with respect—assuming that's a value important to you—is part of your *due diligence*, as we'll see in Chapter 9.

Significantly, Ron and I have complimentary skill sets when it comes to running our business. A fair division of labor, based on your respective strengths, is a key factor in choosing *roles*, as we'll see in Chapter 2. Although we didn't articulate it quite this way at the time, we recognized then that Ron brought volumes of legal and client service expertise, as well as a keen legal mind, to our business. I had fewer years of experience as a lawyer, but greater savvy when it came to marketing and networking. When Ron started as a lawyer, there were many ethical prohibitions on lawyer advertising; plus it was deemed "unseemly" for lawyers to market themselves—after all, "we're not selling used cars". When I started, many of those rules had been relaxed; plus, I learned quickly that you were only indispensable to the extent you brought business to a firm. Otherwise, you were an expendable drone.

Ron and I both felt we could learn from each other—that each had a gift, a talent, to bring to the partnership. As a result, we didn't need to compete against each other.

⊶

Why Do You Need The Key Questions?

When Ron and I ultimately joined forces 11 years ago, we had had the mixed blessing of living through—and witnessing—many of the contentious issues that *The Key Questions* raises. We both had clear ideas of what we did and did not want from a business partnership. But we didn't have the benefit of this book to guide us. What we did have was the framework of a partnership agreement, which took us through some of these issues. We also let the conversation take us on its own journey to see what we might uncover. Both of us were gun-shy; we were adamant about not repeating what we had seen and experienced in the past.

As a result of our conversations, we grew to realize that there were three "people" in this conversation: Ron, me, and the business itself, which would have its own needs, independent of Ron's or mine. Eleven years later, we're still here. I think we can call that a success.

Not only are we our own successful partnership, but we have encountered and advised scores of other business partnerships through our law firm, Paltrowitz & Kaufman

LLP. Whether there are two partners, three, four, or more, the reasons partnerships work well (and don't) tend to be the same. Entrepreneurship is an exhilarating ride. But when people get bitten by the entrepreneurial bug, they often don't focus on the fact that doing what they love, and working with a partner to create a business that does what they love, *are two different things.* That's part of the reason why, according to the National Federation of Independent Business, close to 70% of all business partnerships fall apart. The signs of potential disaster are usually pretty clear, if you know what to look for … so why not look? And why not know? If you want to be sure that business partnership is truly the right move for you, answer the Key Questions.

Many business owners we have encountered are so eager to be off and running that they don't want to spend time with these questions. Like creating a prenuptial agreement before a marriage, they have a feeling that asking these questions—and creating the agreement that memorializes their answers—will be the death-knell of the relationship. Nothing could be further from the truth. It isn't the written agreement that causes the rift between partners; it's the underlying issues they don't want to address (which the agreement forces them to) that splits them apart. They're afraid of the answers, so they don't ask the questions. Business owners who bristle at the question, "Are you sure you really want to do this?" are like Shakespeare's "lady [who] doth protest too much". Often, they are so keen to talk themselves *into* the venture (without having thought it through) that they view *any* question as a direct confrontation. Instead, they hide behind false bravado and bark back, "What's the matter— don't you have confidence in us?" Truth is, it's not whether I as an advisor have confidence in them that is paramount; it's whether they have confidence in themselves and in each other. So they avoid taking the time to explore the partnership relationship before jumping in with both feet. They don't want to face the possibility that they might be making a mistake, especially after they have gone out on a limb by starting the venture in the first place.

This has come up time and again when advising clients. Years ago, we represented the owners of a new business which had just been established. Ron and I met with them to discuss the terms they wanted for their partnership agreement. We discussed the way in which profits and losses would be divided; who would manage which aspects of the business; how much money each was prepared to contribute to the business ... and then I raised the subject of vacation time.

One of them snorted. "You're joking, right?" he sneered. "Have you really worked with entrepreneurs before? We're just starting a business! This isn't some B.S. hobby! It takes everything to get it off the ground. This is a 24/7 venture!"

"Now hold on a minute!" shouted the other, visibly agitated. "I just left a g-ddamned sweatshop. I haven't had a vacation with my wife and kids for four years. I'll be damned if I have to work twice as hard as where I was *in addition to* taking a cut in pay to get this off the ground!"

The shouting match continued, but I needn't have been in the room. From that point on, I was irrelevant. What we had just unearthed for them was that one partner was 24/7; the other was 9-to-5. And the two lifestyles were sufficiently incompatible that no written partnership agreement could paper over the resentment that was bound to fester. They left my office, fuming, and never finished the partnership agreement. Ultimately, they decided not to continue the business together. Belatedly, and begrudgingly, one of them e-mailed me to let me know. "I guess I need to thank you," it read. "I'm pissed off that the situation didn't work out ... but you saved us a lot of time, money, and headaches down the road." In my business, that kind of compliment is a Congressional Gold Medal: it weighs heavily and is exceedingly rare.

In this book, you'll find many of the questions Ron and I answered plus many more, gathered over time through our practice, experiences of our clients, and discussions with colleagues (many of whom have marveled at our "staying power"). *The Key Questions* helps create a shared view of your business and a deeper knowledge of yourself and your business partner. It can be used throughout the life of a business partnership. Answering these questions ten years into a partnership (as Ron and I had to do when I got married and wanted to start a family) is as valuable as answering them ten months before you begin it. Your partnership is a living, breathing entity—*expect* these answers to change somewhat over time as your family and lifestyle situations change. These questions also apply regardless of the legal form of your business. The co-owners of your business may take the legal names of partner (for a general partnership), shareholder (for a corporation), or member (for a limited liability company) ... but they are all *partners*, in the sense that you share the profits and losses of the business, as well as your journey through entrepreneurship. An added benefit of this book is that the questions can be useful whether or not the business relationship involves your co-owners. In many cases, they can be applied to strategic alliances, vendors, clients—anything where your relationship involves give-and-take. For example, you may not want to do business with a vendor that uses sweatshop labor, is habitually late in paying its bills, or contributes a portion of its profits to a cause you do not support. These are important questions for setting your own standards and business culture.

⊶

How to Use and Answer the Key Questions

The *Key Questions* can become an important part of your overall business planning. They dovetail with many of the issues you will confront in planning your business such as cash flow, projected revenues, anticipated sources of clients/customers, and internal operations. But they offer more, an added dimension. In the process of exploring "who am I?" and "who is my partner?" you'll find that your business partner will become one of the more important people in your life, and you will share most of your waking hours with him or her. So don't hurry through this process of exploration. Just as you would not want to rush through your business planning process, so, ideally, you'll take whatever time you need to ask yourself and your partner the *Key Questions.* As my mother used to say about my brother's eating habits, "It's not a race!" Better to have taken your time and carefully thought through these issues than to have rushed into it, only to come up against obstacles and problems that you could easily have anticipated.

Over the years, Ron and I have found that certain conditions and actions can help you get the most out of the *Key Questions.*

☞ **Answer the questions for yourself first**. It's crucial that you know your own mind on these matters. There may be some issues that don't matter as much to you. For example, it may be less important which role you play in the business management, as long as the roles are fair. But a deal-breaker for you may be that you cannot earn less than $45,000 per year. Or $145,000 per year. You may be open to suggestion about the impression the office makes on clients, but have a very definite need for the flexibility to work from home to be with your toddler (or aging parent). When you decide which issues are "open" and which ones are a "must," you are less likely to feel yourself manipulated into making agreements and decisions that do not serve your true interests. You also make better decisions when you have set your own priorities. A manipulated decision is not an honest decision ... and can easily breed resentment. The business is a partnership, yes, but there's a delicate balance to be had. Your needs deserve to be met, too, along with those of your partner and the company.

☞ **Find the right environment**. Whether you are sitting with the *Key Questions* on your own or with your partner(s), choose the right setting. As you start (or re-examine) your business, getting out of the office or away from someone's "home turf" can be mentally freeing. This is a time when you and your partners need to feel creative and open to possibility. Physical surroundings can have that effect on us. Find a place that minimizes distractions (such as ringing telephones) or is quiet enough to allow you to think clearly and have a conversation without shouting. Stay away from multi-tasking temptations like e-mail; turn off the PDAs and the BlackBerrys. Also helpful is a location that doesn't have you "on the meter," that is, where you can stay as long as you like.

☞ **Set your parameters**. Especially if both of you are currently working at other jobs, it's important to be mindful of time and other constraints that may weigh on your potential partner. If you're using your lunch hour for these discussions, one or the other of you may not have the flexibility to allow the conversation to stretch to a three-hour meeting. Respect that by setting a clear time frame and having a reasonable agenda. If all you have is an hour, it may be more realistic to expect that you'll thoroughly address one or two questions in a chapter, rather than an entire chapter itself.

☞ **Listen attentively.** As important as it is for you to know your own vision for the company, your partner(s) are entitled to have a say in it, too. In fact, together, you will end up with a vision for the company that will probably be very different from what each of you originally imagined. If all you want is to get your way all the time, you have no need for a business partner. So be open to suggestions. This is where *active listening skills* come into play. Having already answered the *Key Questions* for yourself, now is a time to really hear your partners' answers. Whatever the question, listen to the answer carefully. "Carefully" means that you are *not* formulating your response while the other is talking. It means that you are *not* daydreaming until it's your turn to talk. It means that you are *not* allowing your emotional reactions to take over. Make a quick note of your reactions, for they are important, and then return to your active listening. Star (*) the issue for further discussion. You can always revisit the subject later.

☛ **Leave emotions at the door.** Like any other relationship, business partnerships can unearth many underlying and deeply held beliefs, emotions, and fears. Starting a business has many similarities to having a child, and we sometimes look to our business partners to help deal with the unresolved "partnership" issues of our childhood. Maybe your parents separated when you were young, leaving your mother to raise you herself. So if your partner mentions that she wants to work from home exclusively while her children are young, feelings of resentment, anger, and fear may arise as you conjure up images of regular late nights, little sleep, and shouldering burdens by yourself. Or even without the family background, who wants to get stuck in a relationship that isn't working? Business partners can and do grow apart. Can you end the relationship without having to wallow in the ugly emotions of betrayal, abandonment, and resentment that can accompany a "breakup"? If you discuss these thorny issues in advance (*see* Chapter 10, Agreement), you can approach them with a cooler head.

After all, how fair-minded can you honestly be once a crisis has erupted or a major change requires confronting?

☛ **Use "both/and" thinking.** You have a marvelous opportunity in your hands to create a business in whatever image you choose. It doesn't have to look or behave like any other business to qualify as a success, *however you choose to define success*. Using "both/and" thinking goes hand in hand with active listening and leaving emotions at the door. The partnership needs to have room for all viewpoints. It's not necessarily an either/or proposition. Disagreements need not kill the partnership. They provide an opening for further, deeper dialogue, rather than running down a simple checklist to see how many items you can cross off. Instead of viewing differences of opinion as a stumbling block, a "do-not-pass-Go-do-not-collect-$200" obstacle, ask yourself *"How can we accommodate both of us?"* Keep that perspective at the forefront of your mind. You may feel that having a partner who needs to telecommute is a deal-breaker. With both/and thinking, you can explore other options: Would it be okay if she (or he) worked in the office certain days of the week? Could we have our own mini-day care in the office? If he did work at home exclusively, how can we measure his productivity so that I can feel he's pulling his weight? Is our business of a type (like, perhaps, a graphic design firm) where one person can be the public face and the other can handle the behind-the-scenes service with e-mail and telephone? You may ultimately arrive at the decision that both needs cannot be accommodated, but you will be doing so in a spirit of cooperation, not opposition.

☞ **Take notes.** First and foremost, let the discussion flow naturally. The point of taking notes is to capture the ideas you have in the course of your discussion; to summarize the areas where you and your partner(s) agree or disagree; to note where you've exhausted a topic or where you can delve further. You don't need to painstakingly record each and every aspect of the discussion; if you do, you're not really part of the conversation or actively listening—you're just playing dictation machine. Out of these notes can emerge the basis for your marketing plan (*see* Chapter 1, Goals), your operations manual (*see* Chapter 2, Roles, or Chapter 7, Communication), and your partnership agreement (*see* Chapter 10, Agreement), among other things!

Whether people will be successful business partners depends on personality traits and a host of issues that a business plan often doesn't touch upon. *The Key Questions* is designed to help you uncover many of those issues and situations that often go unnoticed or unaddressed.

As nerve-wracking and discomfiting as the thought of working with a business partner can be (oh, the vulnerability, on so many levels!), a great partner can be your best resource. If you really want your company to go places, you'll get better and faster results through collaboration than you will on your own. Why? Several reasons. First, no one can know everything there is to know about starting, managing, and growing a business. If you had to figure out everything by yourself, you'd be spending a lot of time on your learning curve, and relatively little on the areas that will bring revenue to your company.

Also, a business partner can provide a source of stimulation and creativity. Knives don't sharpen themselves; they need a hard surface. Different viewpoints can yield new insights or perspectives that you might not have had working on your own. Partners can help you expand beyond yourself. It's been said that every businessperson has an average of 300 contacts in her Rolodex. If you're alone, you have only a set number of people to contact; with a partner, you have just doubled your network.

Finally, partners offer intellectual companionship. Entrepreneurship can be a lonely road, one not understood by those who have not walked its path. It's easy to feel alone and isolated in your endeavors. Business partners can alleviate that isolation. And let's not forget about the benefits of *lunch*! They provide opportunities to celebrate even the small victories. The entrepreneurial road is a rewarding one, in so many ways, but can be long and difficult, too. You can't put a price tag on someone who truly enables you to "keep the faith". Remember the old proverb: "A joy shared is doubled; a problem shared is halved."

Chapter 1

GOALS

The reason most people never reach their goals is that they don't define them.... Winners can tell you where they are going, what they plan to do along the way, and who will be sharing the adventure with them.

—Denis Watley

Many people feel that business partners need to be exactly aligned on every aspect of the business to make the relationship work. Actually, the reverse tends to be truer: As the adage goes, "if the two of you agree on everything, one of you is redundant." We are often challenged to reach greater heights by someone who is not our clone. And in the end, it's not whether you share a love for balance sheets or the same marketing tactics that will make your business succeed. What's crucial is that you see eye-to-eye on the same core goals and values.

People have underlying motivations for starting their own business that need to be uncovered. For example, there may be a need for control, prestige, freedom, security, or a desire to express one's own creativity that is at the heart of one's entrepreneurial quest. If that's the case (and it often is), knowing those underlying goals is crucial to a happy partnership. That's why taking the time to talk through your visions and desires for the business— and what you want it to do for you personally—is so vital. Your business partnership will be sustained through difficult times if you establish a strong foundation at the outset. This is not just a foundation of communication, which we address in more depth in Chapter 7. It's also a foundation of *expectations*, a set of assumptions on which you and your partner(s) will rely as you move forward. This foundation provides the ground rules that will define your business relationship.

As the French author and aviator, Antoine de Saint-Exupery once wrote about love, "[It] consists not in gazing at each other, but in standing shoulder-to-shoulder, gazing in the same direction." Business success is much the same. Entrepreneurs want to know that they are using their time at work to create something meaningful, that has staying power, and that their business partners share that same driving force and vision. Shared goals and values, which these questions will guide you to uncover, are the cornerstones of solid partnerships.

1. What are our personal feelings about entrepreneurship? Why do we really want to do this?

2. Is this a first career for either one of us? First business? Retirement business?

3. Do we have professional goals, separate and apart from our being business owners, that we would like to achieve? For example, do we want to use the business as a platform for advancing a cause or issue? What do we want the business to be able to do for us? What opportunities for creative expression (e.g., writing, public speaking) do we want to get from the business?

4. Why were we dissatisfied with our previous jobs (or current situation)? What did we like about them that we might want to incorporate into our own company?

5. Where do we want this business to be in 3, 5, 10 years? Are we aligned on growth plans (including hiring, regional expansion, etc.) and possible exit strategies? Do we want to build the company for life or build it to sell?

What is our (individual and shared) vision for the business and its future ownership and control?

6.   How do we want to handle the company's earnings? Do we want to put earnings back into the business or do we want to distribute them to the partners for their personal goals?

7.   What are our individual expectations of each other? Do we have similar views of what is realistic to ask of each other?

8.   How will we measure success? How will we gauge progress?

9.   How do we each deal with change? Do we need logical reasons for making a change, such as seeing how it fits into a vision for the future? Are we "adrenaline junkies," feeding off constant change?

10. Why do I need a business partner? What role will the partner play? What can I do with a business partner that I can't do with employees or outsourced help?

Chapter 2

ROLES

All the world is a stage

And all the men and women merely players.

They have their exits and entrances;

Each man in his time plays many parts.

—William Shakespeare

A business has its own existence, separate from its owners. And just like a baby, a business has many needs—all of which must be met for its health and survival. If a baby isn't fed, changed, or given the right inoculations against disease, it can suffer and die. Similarly, if a business doesn't generate new customers, develop payment terms, or have insurance, it too can suffer and die. As proud "parents", or owners, of this new company, it's your responsibility to make sure that these needs are met. But who is equipped to do what, and how can you make sure that the division of labor is fair?

In my law partnership, Ron and I have made subtle divisions of labor that are based as much on our individual character traits as on our talents. As I am more quick-tempered and emotional than Ron, I often leave the difficult confrontations to him. This usually means that he will handle the telephone calls to clients who have been delinquent in paying their bills, or client cases that involve court appearances and arguing before a judge or jury. I am a bit of a compulsive, yet organized, pack rat (I like to call it "meticulous"), able to find invoices, checks, and equipment warranties on a moment's notice—things for which Ron has no patience. So I'm the one who usually handles the accounts payable, able to endure the frustration of jumping through hoops from call center to call center to track down why a particular item has shown up on our credit card statement.

How can you come to a sensible division of labor? By acknowledging the strengths and weaknesses of each partner. This is where self-knowledge and brutal honesty come into play. Business owners have a tendency to believe that they are good at everything when that's just not the case. As a result, they end up getting themselves mired in areas of the business where they create more problems than they solve. Be up-front about your likes and dislikes, where you have experience, and where you are a novice. If you absolutely detest writing checks and balancing bank statements, and can't tell a general ledger from a P&L, handling and overseeing the financial aspects of the company might not be the best thing for you ... or your partner or the business. If you're simply inexperienced but intent on learning about it (which is an admirable trait), a better approach might be for you to take a few courses on financial management, and then gradually work your way into it, under the tutelage of your business partner. The questions below will help you sort through where your skills and personality can be put to best use for the business.

Another point to keep in mind is that roles do—and often must—change. As the business grows, it may no longer be appropriate or feasible for the partners to be as hands-on with certain roles. Or, their personal objectives may change. For example, if one partner undergoes a lifestyle change (e.g., because of a spouse's need to relocate for her job), he may need to work remotely, which might require a shift in roles. As a result, he may need to delegate some of his roles to the other partner(s), to an employee, or to an outside vendor. Therefore, it's important that partners are able to rely on each other to fulfill their chosen roles while leaving enough flexibility to embrace a change, should that occur. The following questions should help you identify the benefits and impediments that each partner brings to the different facets of your company.

1.   What qualifications and experience does each of the owners bring to the business? What assets and resources? Money? Technical expertise? Management talents? Sales skills? Customers/clients? Contacts in the industry (either selling or manufacturing)?

2.   Does one partner have the intellectual property (e.g., a recipe, software program, etc.) that the business needs in order to run?

3.   On what tasks would (or does) each of us spend time? On what areas does each of us *like* to spend time? If money were no object, how would we ideally want to spend our time in the business? What do we like to do least? Most? What do we like to do vs. what do we need to do? Can we

work out a division of labor (both the drudge-work and the fun tasks) that's *fair*?

4.   How would we evaluate our personal business skills, such as oral presentation skills, written communication skills, computer skills, word-processing skills, fax/e-mail experience, organizational skills? How would we evaluate our partner's? If there are weaknesses, how will we address this?

5.   What are our strengths and weaknesses? What are the gaps left open that our skills (together) do not satisfy? Are there gaps in:

- Sales skills, such as pricing, buying, sales planning, negotiating, direct-selling to buyers, customer service follow-up, managing other sales reps, and tracking competitors

- Marketing skills, such as advertising/promotion or public relations, annual marketing plans, media planning and buying, advertising copywriting, marketing strategies, distribution channel planning, pricing, packaging

- Financial planning skills, such as cash-flow planning, monthly financial reporting, bank relationships, and management of credit lines

- Accounting skills, such as bookkeeping, billing (payables and receivables), monthly profit and loss statements/balance sheets, and quarterly/annual tax preparation

- Administrative skills, such as scheduling, payroll handling, and benefits administration

- Personnel management skills, such as hiring employees, firing employees, motivating employees, general management skills

- Technological skills, such as comfort level with word processing, spreadsheet, database, and time management software, Internet and other research, and computer equipment/other peripherals like PDAs, BlackBerrys, and cell phones.

6.   If there are gaps, how will we fill them?

Chapter 3

MONEY

A wise man should have money in his head, but not in his heart.

—Jonathan Swift

Money is a lightning rod, the mother lode of most business strife. The lack of money ("inadequate capitalization") is the #1 cause of business failure, and is among the top sources of contention among business partners. Money, and our attitudes toward it, has an impact that far transcends the new business we're creating; often it has been hard-wired into us from a young age ... and equally as often, we're not even conscious of its effects.

Money means different things to different people. For some, it's security; for others, it's power; for still others, it's freedom. And how do we react if we don't have it? Money is one of the most important subjects for business partners to discuss openly, honestly, and deeply; and it's the one area that most business partners don't want to confront. It brings up all sorts of awkward and unwanted feelings and experiences: terror, vulnerability, manipulation, control,

47

and fear of rejection (or not being good or successful enough), to name a few. The thought of discussing money is about as pleasant as root canal surgery without anesthetic.

What does money mean to us? What happens if what we generate and distribute isn't always proportionate? Few issues raise more hackles than the issue of fairness in money. And business ownership brings to light special financial issues and ethical issues, for a more heightened level of trust is involved than in ordinary business relationships. There's the old joke—which reflects a fear of many entrepreneurs—where the business owner meets with the client and quotes a fee of $500.00. The client asks, "Can I pay cash?" The owner says, "Of course." After the client leaves, the owner counts the money and finds that the client has given her six $100 bills instead of five. The owner realizes she is facing an ethical quandary. What is it? *Do I tell my partner?*

While there's no guarantee you can find out everything you need to know about your partner's attitudes toward money (and whether they'll put their own interests and needs above all else), these questions are a good start.

1.   What are our categories of expense (rent, insurance, utilities, marketing, salaries, etc.)? How much do (or will) we spend monthly, annually, in each category? In one year? Three years? Five years?

2.   What is our ultimate financial goal regarding annual income and when do we anticipate achieving it?

3.   What are our personal financial needs? Can the business generate enough to support itself as well as the partners? Is the company's current income enough to meet our combined needs?

4.   If the business fails to generate enough income to pay us our salaries for a period of time, can we still afford to meet our personal expenses? For how long? What belt-tightening flexibility do we have?

5.   If one partner has a financial need that is greater than another's should that partner be entitled to take more out of the business (even with a possible negative tax effect to the more generous partner)?

6.   What financial (or "capital") contribution will each of us make to the business? Do we have the resources to

make more, if necessary? How much more? Over what period of time?

7.   How will we handle a situation where one partner contributes less than another?

8.   How will we make spending decisions for the company? What kinds of purchases must be jointly decided upon?

9.   Who handles (or oversees) the books and pays the bills? Who handles (or oversees) the long-range financial planning (such as insurance, retirement)? How are these decisions made and who implements/tracks/manages them?

10. Imagine that your company has $5.00 in its account right now. You can either pay a vendor the $5.00 that is owed, or distribute the money to the partners, and make the vendor wait. What would you do? What would your partner do? Do you agree?

11. Imagine that you quoted a project estimate to a client, which the client was perfectly happy to pay in advance. You finished the project in less than the time estimate and under budget. Do you pass along the project savings to the

client? Or do you stick with your original estimate? What would you do? What would your partner do? Do you agree?

Chapter 4

CONTROL

If everything seems under control, you're not going fast enough.

—Mario Andretti

E ntrepreneurs are notorious control freaks. They go into their own business to control their schedules and their destiny. As there's so much uncertainty in the world of business, they also try to control the way in which their company operates. They want to control their employees and make them perform a certain way. And, not surprisingly, they want a certain measure of control over their business partners.

Control, and controlling behavior, can be a good thing— to a degree. Keeping things under control, by establishing reporting and accountability systems, is a good way to measure your company's growth. However, unlike Mae West's quip, "too much of a good thing is wonderful," being too controlling in your business-partner relationship can destroy it. There's a reason you chose to take on a business partner; partly, you didn't want to go it alone. When you bring someone else into the mix, you have to allow their imprint to affect the company in addition to your own.

When you start a company with other people, you need to leave your ego at the door, to some extent. Like two parents raising a child, if you insist on having your own way and having your parenting style followed all the time, the other will begin to feel unappreciated and may well cease contributing to the child-rearing, which then places more burden on you, which makes you more resentful and demanding, which makes the other want to contribute less, and ... You see where this is leading. Running a business is no different. Unless your business partner is doing something truly detrimental to the business (such as having one's paws in the company till), it's crucial to work out your leadership and decision-making styles and processes at the outset.

In running a business, disagreements are inevitable. Ignoring them only makes the situation worse, because time elapses and positions become entrenched. However, a disagreement needn't turn into a shouting match or create a fundamental rift in your company. By discussing in advance *how* you will arrive at certain decisions, you can avoid the acrimony that comes with the disappointment of not getting your own way. In other words, you can disagree without being disagreeable.

At some point, a decision will need to be made. The buck has to stop somewhere. While it's tempting to create a set of egalitarian co-CEO structures, they often do not run practically or efficiently. Think of it: two people having the same position, with the same authority to act on behalf of the company, but with different views on how to handle an issue. Ultimately, you both can't have your own way; someone has to have the final say. Someone has to be in charge. But leadership need not be unlimited or unconditional—or based on a rigid hierarchy. Leadership based on expertise, rather than raw power, often works best. Ask yourselves these questions to learn more about your leadership styles and needs.

1. Can I share management with another? Am I okay with not controlling or having the final say? Are there parts of the business where I absolutely *must* have final say? What if we both want it? How will we overcome the impasse?

2.   What position will we each, as owners, hold? What will your role in the business be, and what do you expect mine to be? Will one person have the ultimate decision-making capacity?

3.   Is there a need for one of us to actually be a leader? Who will it be and in which contexts? Will leadership vary, depending on the context? How will leadership be handled? What will we do if we disagree with the way the other is leading?

4.   Do we share similar views and practices regarding accounting and expense control, time-keeping and record-keeping, productivity and efficiency?

5.   Do we have compatible ways of making decisions and solving problems? Am I focused more on the bottom line and striving to be objective or am I focused on trying to achieve consensus and be inclusive? What about my partner? What does it mean if our styles are different?

6.   How do I express disagreement? Do I take it personally? What is my arguing style? Combative? Withdrawal/silent treatment? Do I have to get my way? Do I capitulate easily? What is my partner's arguing style?

7. How will we handle disagreements on the profound issues facing the company, such as whether to develop multiple streams of business, and if so, which one(s)? How will we handle disagreements on what the company's priorities should be? Is there a way to negotiate a solution that meets both needs? Am I committed to trying to find such a solution, or does "winner take all?" What about my partner?

Chapter 5

VALUES

Happiness is that state of consciousness which proceeds from the achievement of one's values.

—Ayn Rand

W hat do we hold dear? What standards do you hold for your life? What are your values? What qualities and attitudes do you need to see in those with whom you will work closely?

Your values are your beliefs about what is important in life. Values come from a number of sources: family, friends, society, the media, religion, and spiritual traditions. They help shape our attitudes, choices, and actions. Values probably represent the one significant area where incompatibility or clashing with your business partner is the simplest recipe for disaster.

Your values (your beliefs about what is good, right, and desirable) and your value system (the ways in which you prioritize and make decisions based on your values) provide the foundation for your personal and professional judgments and choices. Some values have a greater action-oriented focus, such as achieving money, security, or power; others have a greater spiritually-oriented focus, such as acting honestly, respecting other people, and valuing family. The business will be imprinted with your values. Will you be proud of what it says?

In addition to the lifestyle considerations we'll address in Chapter 6, it's important to know where our business partners "live". Where do their hearts and souls reside? This is an important aspect of compatibility. You may come from totally different communities, but if you agree on the importance, say, of spending time with family, then you are far less likely to be resentful if the other takes time to be with them during the holidays. These questions will help you see the ways in which your respective values shape how you want to express yourselves as business owners. The key is to focus less on whether you act out your values in exactly the same way to the same degree, and more on whether you can abide by the choices that the other partner makes.

1.   Were either of you born into an ethnic or religious community? What place do spiritual and/or religious beliefs play in your personal life? Does religious

observance affect your work schedule? What role if any, does this community play in your life? Is it one where you feel comfortable reaching out to people to advertise your business? If not, why not?

2.   Do we belong to or support (with money and/or time) any charities or causes?

3.   Will we want the company to take on *pro bono* work for the organizations or causes we are involved in? If so, what dollar or time limits do we want to establish? Are there certain causes that we would not want to support (or have the company support)?

4.   What are our views on some of the thornier business issues: Will we outsource overseas? Will we employ illegal immigrants? How will we handle conflicts of interest?

5.   What are our views on what it means to have a "quality of life"? Are those views similar or compatible?

6.   What does "customer service" mean to us? Are our views of serving customers the same or complementary? Does it have the same meaning and importance to both of us?

7.   What are our needs and boundaries when it comes to our personal privacy and confidentiality? The company's needs and boundaries? What do privacy and confidentiality mean to each of us? Does it mean the same thing? How will we handle privacy or boundary issues, or violations of confidentiality, even if made innocently?

8.   What does honesty mean to both of us?

9.   How important is integrity within the partnership?

10.   Do we operate with the same level of intensity? Do we have the same sense of urgency about the same things? How do we feel about meeting deadlines? About paying bills timely?

11.   Do I like my partner? Do I respect my partner? Do I feel my partner respects me? How is that respect shown? Do I respect my partner's contributions, if different from mine? Am I competitive with the contributions made, if the same as mine?

Chapter 6

LIFE/WORK STYLE

Work joyfully and peacefully, knowing right thoughts and right efforts will inevitably bring about right results.

—James Allen

"All work and no play makes Jack a dull boy," goes the old expression. Regardless of the Herculean effort and number of hours a new business can require, entrepreneurs are not automatons that can keep "going and going" without rest, like an Energizer® bunny. Family—and even the basic need to rest and recharge our batteries—requires time outside of work, as does physical exercise, play, service to others (in the form of volunteer work), and spiritual reflection. It's crucial to know exactly what you can expect from your business partner. Are you on the same page when it comes to devoting time to the business?

Lifestyle changes, too, can throw a wrench in the works, especially if they are totally unanticipated. Some business owners are fortunate to have an extensive support system so that having a child (or children) does not adversely affect the time and effort they can devote to the business.

Or, put another way, others may prefer to spend more time with their children, once they come into the picture (whether by birth or adoption). Others may face difficult family situations. Does either one of you have significant family obligations (such as caring for an elderly parent) that limit the amount of time you can be in the office? It is important to prepare for it by discussing your beliefs about them early on in the business relationship.

Our attitudes toward work and priorities are often shaped by our families of origin. While neither of you may be qualified to act as therapist to the other, it is important to be aware of the touchstones that can unearth resistance or negative reactions in the context of this pressure-cooker that is a business relationship. For example, if you have a parent who was a workaholic, you may believe that this is the one true sign of dedication and commitment to the job. But your business partner may have felt deprived of attention from her workaholic father and instead, wants to invest a fair amount of time to be with her children. Can you separate your feelings from your partner's needs?

Another issue that burbles below the surface has to do with giving and receiving criticism. We cannot grow as business owners without some degree of conflict and tension, and it is often the uncomfortable situations that give us the greatest opportunity for personal growth. I think of the time that I was thrust last minute into the lead counsel position for a client's arbitration hearing. My heart was in my mouth virtually every day (not to mention my stomach in knots), but I could never have learned what I did from a book, or from a story Ron recounted of his own experiences. And I certainly could not have done it without his careful and measured tutelage from the sidelines. I was fortunate that he understood me well enough to know how to guide me through this situation. It took a delicate balance of straight talk, a firm hand, and gentle coaxing. But not every learning experience (and partner criticism) is given in a form that we're receptive to hearing. Ferocious feelings can be provoked by a partner's criticisms or judgments. Answering the questions below can help you and your partner clarify feelings about such important topics as ambition, expectations of support, and commitment to your own and to your partner's professional goals.

1.   What kinds of working hours are we planning to keep? Is one of you 24/7 while the other is 9-5? Are you early birds? Late risers? What kind of hours do you ideally want to work? If pressed, can you work more? For what length of time?

2.   Do we care if we work the same hours (if a retail store, could be a problem; if a consulting firm, may not be as much of an issue)? Does the business need us to do so?

3.   How available do we want to be to each other? Outside of the office, how much of our time are we willing to put into work? Generally, are we inclined to bring work home? How much of our time is spent working at home? Do we work at home exclusively? If so, how can we make sure we are accountable to the other (and to the company) for meeting all of the company's (and our clients') needs?

4.   Is your idea of a vacation switching from sales to marketing, while your partner's is nine weeks on the Riviera?

5.   What is your business style? Do you run it with military precision? Are you more relaxed, go-with-the-flow? Do you work better alone or with a team? Are you

task-oriented or relationship-oriented? Detail-oriented or big-picture thinker? Do you perform well under pressure or do you fold? How forgiving are you with mistakes and deviations from your style? Is the other's style one that works for you?

6.   Does either one of us have health concerns (e.g., chronic conditions such as high blood pressure, diabetes, asthma, or other hereditary illness)? Do any of our family members have health concerns? If so, how does that affect your ability to be available for work? For the company's needs? For outside functions for the company? What kinds of accommodations might the company need to make for you?

7.   Do either of the partners have children? If so, will there be regular times when you cannot be in the office? If you plan to have children, when might this occur? How many children do you want to have? Will you want to be able to take time off from work, or work a reduced schedule? For how long?

8.   If one of us needs to make a lifestyle change (new baby, ailing parent, health challenges) that would

temporarily reduce our ability to work, would that be OK? For what period of time? Do we anticipate any such lifestyle changes in the foreseeable future? At what point would this situation make us want to revisit how we have structured ownership and control of the company?

9.   Is there an age/life stage difference between us? How will that affect our relationship? Can the business function if one or the other of us takes time off? If so, how much time is OK?

10. When, if ever, do we want to retire? How would we like to spend our retirement? Do we expect to receive some form of annuity or payout over time from the company to help fund our retirement?

11. What baggage about entrepreneurship do we bring to the partnership? Are we the product of entrepreneurial parents? Are we the first entrepreneurs in the family? What messages were we given about entrepreneurs (e.g., "Entrepreneurs are the courageous backbone of the economy" or "There's little difference between self-employed and unemployed.")?

Chapter 7

COMMUNICATION

The most important thing in communication is to hear what isn't being said.

—Peter Drucker

Solid communication is, at a minimum, a two-way street. Yes, there is a "speaker" and a "listener," but that's only half of the story. To have real communication, the speaker must then listen to the listener's feedback. The listener becomes the speaker and the speaker, the listener. Sounds simple enough, yes?

Not always. The speaker needs to convey her information clearly, and the listener needs to hear the information carefully. Otherwise, misunderstandings, mistakes, and gaffes come marching in. And there are myriad reasons why what one says, the other doesn't hear: each may be listening for something else (usually what *we* want to hear), not paying attention, responding negatively to the communication style ... or the information is too little, too late.

In the fast-paced world of business, there is always a risk that business partners will drift apart. They're so busy, focused on the day-to-day of managing the business that it's hard to make the time to step back to reflect on the business and how it is growing. That's where having a check-in process can help. Many partners schedule regular meetings and promise to make that time sacrosanct—no conflicting meetings! Whether it's a conference call or face-to-face meeting or both, this forces business partners to make internal communication a priority. As an added benefit, it prevents dire issues from festering for lack of an airing. Check in with your partners to see if that is a style that works for them: in some cultures, it may be deemed insulting to have to *schedule* a call with one's business partner, rather than the partner's readily making himself available when needed.

It's not only the timing of communication that helps build strong partnerships, but the *manner* in which you communicate. Business partners can get so caught up in making fast decisions that they levy criticism just as directly and quickly. A sharp criticism, like "You're not pulling your weight," is unlikely to be received warmly. Rather, it has the effect of taking a jousting pole and running it through your partner's chest. In turn, your partner will probably not care to listen to your underlying concerns, and instead will focus on ways she can defend herself against your jabs. She's not only formulating a response, she's coming up with a laundry list of *your* faults that she has refrained from expressing until now. You can avoid communication tit-for-tats by understanding each other's communication styles. No doubt, there will be a bit of trial-and-error until you get it right, but if you are able to approach this in a spirit of learning and accommodation, you'll go a long way to solidifying your business relationship.

Communication, especially around making important decisions, is another area where it helps to check your ego at the door. Remember that both partners are in this business together, for the success of all. It doesn't matter who came up with which idea that ultimately got implemented. It's best not to go into a decision-making conversation already having chosen an ideal outcome. If you remain open to brainstorming with your partner, you can create a solution together that surpasses whatever idea either one of you would have come up with individually!

1.   Do we communicate in a similar way? If not, are our styles complementary? Do we prefer to discuss things informally, or have a list of items in advance to give ourselves time to think it through? Do I prefer to listen and talk or read and write?

2.   Do we function well with team meetings? Do we value collaboration? How much is too little? How much is too much?

3.   How often do we feel we need to communicate about what's going on in the business?

4.   How will we communicate if we are in different time zones and/or countries?

5.   How do we let people know when we are upset? If something goes wrong, are we compatible in the way we'll deal with it?

6.   Are we comfortable talking about big issues like trust, confidentiality, fairness, and money?

7.   How was approval or disapproval expressed in our family of origin? Can we accept criticism? Can we accept compliments? Are we able to give constructive criticism to others?

Chapter 8

ENVIRONMENT

Everything that possesses life dies if it has to live in uncongenial surroundings.

—Muhammad Iqbal

Your office environment is where you will be spending the majority of your waking hours. Your office is also a reflection of your business. It is a form of advertising and marketing to your clients, and should be consistent with the kind of image you want to project.

As with our personal living spaces, our office spaces often comprise the single largest business expense for our companies. So it's important to budget carefully and have an open conversation with your partner about the kind of work environment you want to create and *truly* need for your business to grow. The stories are legion of dot-com companies receiving multi-million dollar infusions of capital, and then spending huge portions of it on the trappings—leasing space in the most expensive buildings, with floor-to-ceiling windows, impressive mahogany desks, and large leather chairs ... because that was the style that denoted power. They ended up spending their money before they had a business that fully functioned and could sustain those kinds of expenses.

Entrepreneurs can get caught up in trying to prove themselves according to someone else's rules. Unless you are well-capitalized from the outset, it makes more sense to minimize expenses and not go bananas in the furniture supply store buying the biggest and most expensive of everything. In the cold, hard light of rationality, the suggestion makes sense. But for business owners who have grown up with their own view of what a successful company's office has to look like (because that's what Grandpa's office or Mommy's office looked like), those images can be hard to shake. The result is that without careful discussion, they work their way into your spending plan and can end up over-inflating your budget.

While your office is where you company lives, it is also where *you* work. Whether or not you have the luxury of abundant space, your office needs to shelter both the company and each individual—on all levels. Therefore, you and your partner need to discuss the space you will inhabit together. Open, loft space may feed your sense of freedom, but represent a lack of privacy to your partner. Conversely, cubicles may be cozy to your partner, but claustrophobic to you. The *feng shui* aspects of a harmonious office are equally important: items should be placed within easy reach, with open flowing space for walking around, entertaining clients (if need be), appropriate lighting, and freedom from distractions. All these inspire the right energy and can influence whether you want to come into the office or not.

The same principles apply to any home office that you might need to establish. Especially with a home office, you will face the issues of accountability to the company (how will we know whether you are really getting work done at home?) as well as the practicality of carving out physical space that is free from distractions and interruptions. The following questions will help you identify the surroundings that will work best for you and your partner(s).

1.   Where is (or will be) our office? Describe its geographical location. What kinds of amenities are near the office?

2. What kind of setup do we need? What kind of space needs does the business have? Do we need a showy conference room for entertaining clients? Is bare-bones, just-the-essentials OK? Will we each work virtually, with no central office? If so, where will we hold our meetings with clients? With each other?

3. What impression do you want the office to leave on people who visit? How is that in line with your image of the business overall? Does that impression need to extend to the public areas of the business (e.g., conference rooms)? Should it extend to the private (personal office) areas as well?

4. Will it matter what kind of office space we have? Windowed office? Grade A building? Fancy furniture? What percentage of our monthly income are we prepared to spend on rent on a monthly or annual basis? How much will we spend on furnishings and supplies? What factors are important in making these decisions (price, quality, style)?

5. Who is responsible for keeping the office clean? How much of this do we need to do ourselves? To what extent

can we hire others to do it? Who is responsible for maintaining client files? How will we organize our work, especially if we are working virtually?

6. If the business is already an ongoing concern, what physical space changes will the new owners require?

7. Are we different in terms of our needs for cleanliness/organization? Is one or both of us neat? Messy? A pack rat? An organizational wizard?

8. In what kind of environment do we work best? A competitive, energy-filled environment with lots of external stimulation? A quiet environment that fosters concentration and working without interruption? Are our styles the same? If they differ, can both be accommodated in the same space?

9. If we work at home, how can we set up an efficient system to keep track of client files or materials? Is one of us a Mac person and the other a PC person? Can we network our computers?

Chapter 9

DUE DILIGENCE

A lot of things happen over time. You don't always have a true picture of the landscape early on. Doing your due diligence makes sense.

—Michael Lombardi

Due diligence brings up images of lawyers in gray suits carrying hefty briefcases and poring over stacks upon stacks of papers in archival boxes in a musty room. Your due diligence won't be anywhere near as painful. But there are some tough questions you should ask yourself and ask *about* (not necessarily *of*) your business partners to find out about their past. While precedence is not prophecy, you need to know your partner's history, just as you would want to know about a romantic partner. Has your partner bankrupted a series of businesses in the past? What explanations does your partner give for these business failures? Do the explanations make sense? Or are they more akin to rationalizations? Like romantic relationships, most business partners don't ask these key questions ... and sometimes, they suffer the consequences of a bad choice.

All the other stars may be in alignment, but a little poking around could alert you to serious issues that a face-to-face conversation may not reveal.

Not surprisingly, when embarking upon a business partnership, entrepreneurs often want to put their best foot forward. They operate on the ready assumption that they want the partnership deal to go through, rather than looking at it objectively and asking, "is this a deal that I truly *want* to go forward with?" People often discount the possibility that the answers they receive may not be the answers they want to hear. Can these answers be confirmed from other sources? Or are you relying only on your partner's say-so as to how he would behave in a particular situation? How can you verify that he is telling the truth?

This is an area that many entrepreneurs shy away from. They'll exclaim, "How can I ask these questions? Isn't a business partnership relationship all about trust?" Yes, it's about trust, but it's also about business. Your business partner should not be surprised that you want to get independent corroboration of the statements she is making; she should trust that you are taking these steps *precisely* because you are serious about moving forward, and that you will keep whatever you learn confidential. These are the steps that business people are expected to take. After all, you'd consider checking references before hiring an employee or contractor, wouldn't you? This is your business livelihood, not a casual dalliance. Trust also plays a role *after* you have made the decision to move forward together. *You* need to trust that your business partner is doing the right thing and behaving ethically with regard to the business. If you don't feel that you can run a business with this partner without micromanaging and constantly looking over your shoulder (and hers), then it's not the right fit.

This group of questions is designed to get you to reflect upon your own observations of your business partner. For example, cultural differences can engender misunderstandings, which can blossom quickly into deep fissures. Your partner, at heart, may not have the entrepreneurial fortitude to stick with the business, despite other areas of compatibility. Other questions give you ideas for information you may want to gather from third parties. What you learn need not be a deal-breaker, but it will give you ammunition with which you can better protect your interests in structuring the business and your respective roles in it.

1. Are we products of the same culture? If there are cultural differences, what is considered polite/rude in your culture? Your partner's? Where might the two of you clash?

2. Do you share the same sense of humor? If not, how do you react? Bemusement? Offense?

3. How do different cultures view leadership and accountability—especially if you are coming into an already-ongoing business? Is leadership about rubber-stamping the decisions that have already been made or holding those decisions up to scrutiny? Is accountability an accepted factor or a sign of mistrust?

4. What is your partner's sense of deadlines and time? Is it okay to show up to a 4:00 P.M. appointment at 4:27 P.M.? What do they complete/leave for later?

5. What kind of temper do your partners have? How do they treat their employees? Do they interact well with others?

6. If your partner already has a business of her own, does she pay her landlord, vendors, and employees promptly? Whether or not it will be the business you will work in together, ask to look at the books. How is the business doing? How long has your partner had that business?

7. What is your partner's family background like? Divorce? Children? Drugs? Alcohol? Can your partner financially afford to be in business with you? Do you notice any erratic behavior (which could be the sign of substance abuse or other addiction)?

8. Go out to dinner or on non-business outings with your partner. Can your partner hold a conversation? What is her personality like when socializing? Is she a similar person as when at work, or radically different? Does she drink too much? How are her table manners? How does she treat the wait staff? As a representative of your company, will her demeanor and behavior be an

embarrassment if you're entertaining clients or other business associates?

9.   How does your partner dress? Is his personal style and hygiene in sync with the nature of your business and the image you want to project? Is he well-groomed? Are his shoes in reasonably good condition? Are his fingernails clean (less important, perhaps, for an auto mechanic than a dentist)?

10. How do your partners speak on the telephone to others? How do they speak to their life partners? Do they speak with respect?

11. Does your partner take responsibility for her actions and mistakes? Can you come up with two or three examples?

12. How do you feel when you are with these business partners? Do they make you feel good? Do they gang up on you? Do you feel encouraged to build the business, or do you feel beaten down?

13. What is your partner's spending style and habits? Is your partner impulsive? Does your partner make business or spending decisions without consulting others (when,

perhaps, he should)? What is your partner's credit rating? (Note that lenders are likely to check the credit history of all partners, which could impede your ability to get needed financing).

14. Ask for references. What do your partner's peers say about her? Do they feel your personalities and styles would be compatible? What do her clients say about her business personality and reputation? What about vendors? Do any negative reports show up on Google®?

15. Conduct a background check. Are there any criminal convictions or lawsuits on your partner's record? Any complaints with the Better Business Bureau? Did your partner volunteer this information or did you have to dig it up? What explanations does your partner give for them? Does he have a reputation for lack of integrity?

16. Is your partner self-motivated? What is her attitude toward "hard work" and risk-taking? Does she have a thick skin to withstand entrepreneurial setbacks? For that matter, do you?

17. On a scale of 1 to 10, with 10 being the ideal, how would you rate your business partner in the following

areas: ability to manage risk and stress, family support, ability to deal with failure, ability to work alone, ability to work with and manage others? How would you rate yourself?

Chapter 10

AGREEMENT

Set your expectations high; find men and women whose integrity and values you respect; get their agreement on a course of action; and give them your ultimate trust.

—John Akers

Not enough ink can be spilled and trees felled to remind you that it's not enough to discuss all of these issues: you *must* put your partnership agreement in *writing*. Partnership relationships can blow up in your face and cause lasting damage to your ego, finances, and possibly, reputation, if you do not handle them professionally.

The Hollywood mogul Samuel Goldwyn once said, "A verbal agreement isn't worth the paper it's printed on." Minds change, memories are fallible, history gets "revised". There are all sorts of reasons to put your partnership agreement in writing. Some entrepreneurs are leery of asking their business partners to put it in writing, as if doing so will douse the flame of excitement for the venture. And maybe it will a little bit. But what you trade in ardor and fantasy feelings, you more than make up for in reality and solid foundation. It's like the phase of shifting from that first blush of romantic love/lust to having a tangible, sustainable relationship with its ups and downs. At first, your heart leaps—a business! A business partner to share the peaks and valleys! Oh, joy! Oh, bliss! Visions of dollar signs and perennially happy clients dance in your head. Most businesses, though, don't miraculously materialize and function on that basis alone. There's a necessary step for planning and process. *How* will you serve your customers so that you repeatedly achieve that ecstatic result?

Similarly, *how* will you work with a business partner in a way that sustains those good feelings you had at the outset? What processes can you put into place to ensure a fair division of labor, a fair division of money, a fair division of ownership, and a fair sale price should a partner need to leave the business? If you haven't put these issues to paper, whatever you may have decided previously can be wiped out and set aside. Why? Because when you most accurately need to recall all of the terms of the agreement, you can't. Or when you and you partner most need to see eye-to-eye, you don't. Or because, without a written agreement, the laws of your state that control your business will take over and decide these issues for you ... perhaps very differently from what you and your partner would have wanted.

When working out the details with your business partners, there's one important thing to keep in mind: *a partnership agreement is your friend.* It is an invaluable tool to help you keep track of the significant issues you need to decide and the agreements you have reached. It allows you to make your *own* decisions about how to structure your relationship with your partners ... in your own image. For those concerned about being locked forever into a way of operating, *don't worry*: partnership agreements can be changed at any time—provided the partners agree, of course. A good agreement will include terms on how these changes can be made.

For those who still can't bring themselves to have a partnership agreement, *get over it.* This is business, not playtime in the sandbox. If you're afraid of hurting people's feelings by putting this agreement in writing, then you may seriously want to rethink the whole venture—thin skins don't last long. You'll be putting lots of hard-earned money and time at risk—valuable resources that you may not recoup if the business goes belly-up.

Another benefit to having a partnership agreement is that you will have worked out the thorny issues well in advance of when you need to rely on them. You will have already decided what's fair between you. It should come as no surprise that what's fair changes radically depending on the level of emotional tension in a situation. Years ago, when setting up a separate business venture (not a law firm), I chose a business partner whom I thought would be the perfect match. We had known each other in law school, and were foursquare on many of the *Key Questions.* She was the one who pushed for regular partnership discussions, adding, "We're both attorneys. If we, of all people, don't have a partnership agreement, we're idiots!" The exercise of going through these discussions was grueling. It forced us to imagine scenarios of abandonment and departure … and to decide the fairest way to handle them. If she left the venture before our first product came to market, was she entitled to any ongoing compensation for her efforts? What if the reason she "left" was that she died? Or became disabled? What if I left to pursue other interests? Who should have the rights to the intellectual property that we created jointly? What if *I* left after the first product came to market? Was I entitled to any compensation for future products, given my input in getting the process started? We spent hours trying to come to grips with how we might feel under the various circumstances, and what we believed was a reasonable solution. In the end, we not only had our partnership agreement, but a much stronger personal relationship, forged in the cauldron of these difficult discussions. And when she did need to bow out of the venture for personal reasons a year or so later, we were able to handle it with a minimum of fuss or rancor, precisely because *we had an impartial process already worked out*, which we followed faithfully. To this day, she remains a dear friend.

Do you want to embark on a new venture—and *ad*venture? Start now by stretching your wings and your comfort zone and demanding a partnership agreement. If your partner is the one dragging her feet, *that* can be the red flag to indicate that she doesn't want to be held to the agreement you make. If you can find a partner whose word is his bond, that's nice. But if you find a partner who is also willing to commit that bond to writing, that's priceless. A partner who is really true to his word will have no hesitation indicating up, down, and sideways that he intends to stand by his promises.

What Goes Into a Partnership Agreement?

Partnership agreements can go by different names. If the owners are owners of a business operating as a legal partnership, it's called a *partnership agreement*. If the owners own shares in a corporation, it's called a *shareholders' agreement*. If the owners own membership interests in a limited liability company, it's called an *operating agreement*.

Whatever it's called (and we have been using the term "partner" to refer generally to two or more people owning a business together), the ownership agreement covers the legal issues that underlie a business partnership relationship. Like a prenuptial agreement in the marriage context, a "business prenup" looks at the reasons the partners might want to end the relationship, how they will resolve disputes, how they will own property (in this case, the business itself), and how money and property will change hands in the event of a business "divorce". A competent business attorney can take you through all of the aspects of what should be included. Most carefully thought-out partnership agreements address the following issues (among others):

- The purpose of the business
- Financial (called "capital") contributions
- Ownership percentages
- How profits and losses will be allocated
- Guidelines for management responsibilities
- How major decisions will be made
- Special obligations that the owners owe to the business (such as confidentiality)
- Partner departures (for whatever reason)
- Buyout (also called "buy-sell") provisions, procedures, and prices upon partner departure
- How disputes will be resolved

The buyout provisions are especially important to have in writing. At the point in time that a partner is leaving the business, emotions are highly charged. Partners will remember what they want to remember, particularly if it works in their favor. If the departing partner wants her money right away, chances are that she will recall that the payout terms were "upon departure," rather than "in monthly installments over five years." More urgently, if the partners cannot agree on the procedures and terms for buying back a partner's ownership interest, they may have to go to court to resolve them ... which could result in the total loss of the business.

Buyout provisions in a written agreement are the reminder of how all of you agreed to handle matters fairly, when cooler heads prevailed. By including these provisions regarding the orderly transition of business ownership, you help ensure that there remains a business to transition! These are just a few of the questions an attorney would ask:

1.   How will decisions be made in the company? Is each one of us comfortable with the other making decisions in

areas where we have not been consulted? If not, what areas are they? Do we need 2/3 majority or unanimity on certain issues? If so, what issues are they?

2.   How long do we expect, or would we like, our partnership to last? Are we willing to commit to staying with the business for a certain minimum amount of time?

3.   How will we split up ownership, how will we divide profits and losses, and how will we each be paid?

4.   May the partners have outside business interests or other employment while owning the company? May partners work for a competing business after they leave the company?

5.   Who will have the authority to execute legal and financial (including bank check) documents on behalf of the company?

6.   How many vacation, sick, and personal days should partners be entitled to take each year? Will that depend on the number of years of service?

7.   What kind of conduct would lead you to want to fire or get rid of a partner? Company theft? Illegal substance use? Sexual harassment of employees or vendors?

8.   What if a partner gets an outside offer to purchase her ownership interest in the company? Should the company get the first opportunity to match the offer (called "right of first refusal")?

9.   What is the buyout procedure for a partner who wants to resign or retire?

10. What if a partner gets sick or is temporarily (less than six months) disabled? Will he be paid a regular salary? For how long? What about a longer-term disability?

11. How will we value the business when a partner wants to leave?

Acknowledgments

As I have tried to emphasize throughout *The Key Questions*, no man (or woman) is an island. I could not have written this book without the insights and assistance of others. Special thanks go to Jaime Giraldo, Angela Cason, Helen Poon, and my Starbucks table-mate Michael for sharing their perspectives on and experiences (both good and ill) in their own business partnerships, and to Janet Anderton and Judy Gitenstein for their invaluable feedback and support. I also want to thank the many clients of Paltrowitz & Kaufman LLP, who have honored us with their business and let us help them build successful partnerships.

Finally, one cannot be a "partner" by oneself. It takes two to tango. I am supremely grateful to my business partner, Ronald Paltrowitz, who took a chance on me years ago and gave me the opportunity to fly.

Nina L. Kaufman
New York City

About the Author

With the meteoric rise in small business ownership, there's a vital need for lawyers who can "speak English" and truly address the entrepreneurial experience. Enter Nina Kaufman. A prolific writer, legal blogger, and attorney to small businesses, Nina is the founder and president of Wise Counsel Press LLC which publishes user-friendly and affordable guides and teleclasses on legal issues for entrepreneurs. She is also the co-founding partner of Paltrowitz & Kaufman LLP, a boutique law firm that helps NYC-based small businesses get started and grow. Nina has written numerous articles on a wide range of legal topics that have appeared in publications including the *New York Enterprise Report*, *Enterprising Woman*, *WomenandBiz.com*, and *TheSquare.com*, in addition to her own monthly e-newsletter, *Words to the Wise*, and *Business Partnership Central* blog. She also authors the

Business Law Advisor column and *Making It Legal* blog for *WomenEntrepreneur.com.*

An educator with a sense of humor, Nina is also a sought-after professional speaker (and occasional stand-up comedienne!) who has given seminars, workshops, and presentations on small business legal issues for numerous organizations in the New York City area. Nina has been featured in the *Wall Street Journal*, *SmallBusiness Computing.com*, *Ecommerce-Guide.com*, the *American Bar Association Journal*, *The New York Law Journal*, and *Entrepreneur* magazine, and has appeared on Fox Channel 5's Good Day NY program.

To learn more about Nina's work, visit www.WiseCounsel Press.com, www.palkauf.com, and www.BusinessPartner shipCentral.com.